Breakfast Anytime

Breakfast Bests – Morning, Noon or Night

Printed in the United States of America
by G&R Publishing Co.

Published By:

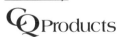Products

507 Industrial Street
Waverly, IA 50677

ISBN-13: 978-1-56383-303-8
ISBN-10: 1-56383-303-4
Item #7029

Table of Contents

Breakfast Anytime

Omelets, Frittatas & Scrambled Eggs

Tortilla Egg Scramble

Ingredients

2 T. butter or margarine
10 eggs
½ C. evaporated milk
½ tsp. ground cumin
2 C. coarsely broken tortilla chips
1 C. shredded Cheddar cheese
Salt and pepper to taste
2 T. chopped fresh cilantro (optional)
Salsa, warmed (optional)

Directions

Melt butter in a large skillet over medium heat. In a large bowl, beat eggs, evaporated milk and cumin then add to skillet. Cook, stirring frequently to scramble, until eggs start to set. Sprinkle egg mixture with tortilla chips and cheese. Season with salt and pepper. Continue to cook, stirring often, until eggs are cooked through. If desired, sprinkle with cilantro and serve with warmed salsa.

Baked Mexican Omelet

Makes 4 servings

Ingredients
½ C. salsa
1 C. shredded Monterey Jack cheese
1 C. shredded Cheddar cheese
6 eggs
1 C. sour cream
Salt and pepper to taste

Directions
Preheat oven to 350°. Spread salsa over bottom of a
10″ pie plate. Sprinkle cheeses evenly over salsa. In a
medium bowl, beat eggs then blend in sour cream. Pour
egg mixture over cheeses. Season with salt and pepper.
Bake for 30 to 40 minutes or until eggs are set.

Feta Scrambled Eggs

Makes 8 servings

Ingredients
2 T. butter or margarine
½ C. chopped onion
8 eggs
½ C. chopped tomatoes
¼ C. crumbled feta cheese
Salt and pepper to taste

Directions
Melt butter in a large skillet over medium heat. Sauté onion until translucent. In a medium bowl, beat eggs then pour into skillet. Cook, stirring frequently to scramble, until eggs start to set. Add chopped tomatoes and feta cheese then season with salt and pepper. Continue cooking, stirring occasionally, until cheese melts.

Scrambled Eggs with Crab & Chives

Makes 6 servings

Ingredients
6 T. butter or margarine, divided
½ C. finely chopped red bell pepper
½ lb. fresh lump or jumbo crabmeat, flaked
2 T. minced fresh chives or green onion
9 eggs
5 T. heavy or whipping cream, divided
½ tsp. salt
¼ tsp. pepper

Directions
Melt 2 tablespoons butter in a large skillet over medium heat. Add bell pepper and cook for approximately 3 minutes or until tender. Add crabmeat and cook for approximately 2 minutes or until heated through. Transfer mixture to a bowl and stir in chives. Cover to keep warm. Melt another 2 tablespoons butter in the skillet over medium heat. In a medium bowl, beat together eggs and 2 tablespoons cream. Add egg mixture to skillet and cook, stirring frequently to scramble, until eggs are almost set. Add remaining 3 tablespoons cream, 2 tablespoons butter, salt and pepper. Cook until thick and creamy then stir in crabmeat mixture.

Veggielicious Scrambled Eggs

Ingredients

¼ C. olive oil
¼ C. chopped green bell pepper
¼ C. sliced fresh mushrooms
¼ C. chopped onion
6 eggs
¼ C. milk
¼ C. chopped tomato
¼ C. shredded Cheddar cheese

Directions

Heat olive oil in a large skillet over medium-high heat. Add bell pepper, mushrooms and onion then sauté until onion is translucent. In a medium bowl, beat together eggs and milk. Add egg mixture to skillet then stir in tomato. Cook until eggs are almost set before stirring in cheese.

Scrambled Egg Cups

Makes 6 servings

Ingredients

½ lb. bulk pork sausage
12 eggs
½ C. chopped onion
¼ C. chopped green bell pepper
½ tsp. salt
¼ tsp. pepper
¼ tsp. garlic powder
½ C. shredded Cheddar cheese

Directions

Preheat oven to 350°. In a large skillet over medium-high heat, crumble and cook sausage until browned; drain grease and set aside. In a medium bowl, beat eggs then stir in onion, bell pepper, salt, pepper and garlic powder. Mix in sausage and cheese. With a ⅓ measuring cup, spoon mixture into greased muffin cups. Bake for 20 to 25 minutes until eggs are set, being careful not to over-bake.

Ham & Cheese Baked Omelet

Makes 5 servings

Ingredients
8 eggs
1 C. milk
½ tsp. seasoning salt
½ C. diced ham
½ C. shredded Cheddar cheese
½ C. shredded mozzarella cheese
1 T. dried minced onion

Directions
Preheat oven to 350°. In a medium bowl, beat together eggs and milk. Stir in seasoning salt, ham, cheeses and dried onion. Pour mixture into a greased 8 x 8″ baking dish. Bake for 40 to 45 minutes or until eggs are set.

Omelet in a Mug

Makes 1 serving

Ingredients
2 eggs
2 T. shredded Cheddar cheese
2 T. diced ham
1 T. diced green bell pepper
Salt and pepper to taste

Directions
In a greased microwave-safe mug, beat eggs. Stir in cheese, ham and bell pepper. Season with salt and pepper. Microwave, uncovered, on high power for 1 minute. Stir then continue to cook for another 1 to 1½ minutes or until eggs are set.

13

Light Veggie Omelet

Ingredients

1 egg
3 egg whites
1 T. grated Parmesan cheese
1 T. shredded Cheddar cheese
¼ tsp. salt
⅛ tsp. pepper
⅛ tsp. crushed red pepper flakes
⅛ tsp. garlic powder
½ tsp. olive oil
½ C. sliced fresh mushrooms
2 T. finely chopped green bell pepper
1 T. finely chopped onion
1 C. torn fresh spinach

Directions

In a medium bowl, beat egg and egg whites. Mix in cheeses, salt, pepper, red pepper flakes and garlic powder; set aside. In a medium skillet, heat olive oil over medium-high heat. Sauté mushrooms, bell pepper and onion for approximately 5 minutes or until tender. Reduce heat to medium and add spinach. Cook, stirring often, until spinach is wilted. Add egg mixture. As eggs set, lift edges to allow uncooked eggs to flow underneath until all eggs are set.

Denver Omelet

Ingredients
1 tsp. butter, divided
2 T. julienne-cut green bell pepper
2 T. julienne-cut red bell pepper
¼ C. sliced onion
¼ C. diced ham
¼ C. sliced fresh mushrooms
3 eggs
⅛ tsp. salt
1 pinch pepper
2 T. shredded sharp Cheddar cheese
Sour cream (optional)

Directions
Melt ½ teaspoon butter in a medium skillet over medium-high heat. Add bell peppers, onion, ham and mushrooms to skillet and sauté for approximately 5 minutes or until onion is translucent. Transfer the mixture to a bowl and set aside. In a small bowl, beat together eggs, salt and pepper until just combined. Melt the remaining ½ teaspoon butter in the skillet over medium heat. Pour the egg mixture into the skillet and tilt pan to spread the egg mixture evenly. Cook until eggs are almost set then sprinkle ham mixture and cheese over all. Fold in half and, if desired, serve with sour cream.

Santa Fe Frittata

Makes 4 servings

Ingredients

6 eggs
¼ C. milk
4 tsp. vegetable oil, divided
2 sausage patties, thawed and cut into ¼" to ½" pieces
1 C. julienne-cut red or green bell pepper
½ C. canned black beans, rinsed and drained
½ C. shredded Monterey Jack, Pepper Jack
    or Cheddar cheese
Sliced avocado, sliced green onions,
    sour cream or salsa (optional)

Directions

Preheat oven broiler. In a medium bowl, beat together
eggs and milk; set aside. Heat 2 teaspoons oil in a large
oven-proof skillet over medium heat. Add sausage pieces
and bell pepper; cook until sausage is heated through and
peppers are just tender. Stir in black beans and remaining
2 teaspoons oil. Add egg mixture to skillet. As eggs cook,
lift edges to allow uncooked eggs to flow underneath
until all eggs are almost set. Sprinkle cheese over eggs
then broil 5" from heat for 2 to 3 minutes or until
eggs are set and cheese is melted. If desired, serve with
avocado, onions, sour cream or salsa.

Taco Frittata

Ingredients
½ lb. lean ground beef
1 tsp. minced onion
½ pkg. taco seasoning
¼ C. water
10 eggs
1 C. shredded Cheddar cheese
Tortilla chips
Shredded lettuce
Salsa

Directions
In a medium skillet over medium-high heat, cook ground beef and onion until beef is browned; drain grease. Add taco seasoning and water then simmer for 2 minutes. In a medium bowl, beat eggs and pour over meat mixture. Turn heat to low and cover pan. Cook for 10 to 12 minutes or until eggs are almost set. Sprinkle with cheese and cover skillet until cheese melts. To serve, cut frittata into wedges and top each with tortilla chips, shredded lettuce and salsa.

Spinach-Potato Frittata

Makes 6 servings

Ingredients

2 T. olive oil
6 small red potatoes, sliced
1 C. torn fresh spinach
2 T. minced green onions
1 tsp. crushed garlic
1 small tomato, diced
Fresh basil, chopped (optional)
Salt and pepper to taste
6 eggs
⅓ C. milk
½ C. shredded Cheddar or mozzarella cheese

Directions

Heat olive oil in a medium skillet over medium heat. Place sliced potatoes in the skillet, cover and cook for approximately 10 minutes or until potatoes are tender but still firm. Mix in spinach, green onions, garlic, tomato and, if desired, basil. Season with salt and pepper. Cook, stirring occasionally, for 1 to 2 minutes until spinach is wilted. In a medium bowl, beat together eggs and milk. Pour egg mixture over vegetables in skillet. Sprinkle with cheese and reduce heat to low. Cover and continue cooking for 5 to 7 minutes or until eggs are set and cheese is melted.

Crab Frittata

Ingredients
2 T. olive oil
1 clove garlic, minced
⅔ C. chopped onion
1 C. chopped zucchini
½ C. sliced fresh mushrooms
3 eggs
½ C. milk
¼ tsp. pepper
¼ C. grated Parmesan cheese
8 oz. fresh lump or jumbo crabmeat, flaked

Directions
Preheat oven to 350°. Heat olive oil in a large skillet over medium heat. Sauté garlic, onion, zucchini and mushrooms until tender. In a medium bowl, beat together eggs, milk, pepper and cheese. In a greased 1½ quart baking dish, layer crabmeat, vegetable mixture and egg mixture. Bake for 20 to 25 minutes or until eggs are set.

Ramen Noodle Frittata

Makes 4 servings

Ingredients
2 (3 oz.) pkgs. chicken flavored Ramen noodles
6 eggs
2 tsp. butter
½ C. shredded Cheddar cheese

Directions
In a medium pan of boiling water, place Ramen noodles, reserving the seasoning packets. Cook until tender then drain water. In a medium bowl, beat together eggs and seasoning from noodles. Mix in cooked noodles. Melt butter in a large skillet over medium heat. Add egg mixture and cook for approximately 5 minutes. Flip egg mixture, sprinkle cheese over eggs and cook for approximately 2 more minutes or until cheese melts.

Parmesan Frittata

Makes 6 servings

Ingredients

3 T. vegetable oil

2½ C. frozen shredded hash browns

2 C. mixed fresh vegetables, such as small
broccoli florets, chopped bell peppers
and shredded carrots

8 eggs

3 T. milk

¼ tsp. salt

⅓ C. grated Parmesan cheese

Directions

Heat oil in a large skillet over medium-high heat. Sauté hash browns and the vegetables of your choice for approximately 5 minutes, stirring occasionally, or until potatoes are browned and vegetables are tender. In a medium bowl, beat together eggs, milk and salt. Pour egg mixture evenly over vegetables. Cover and reduce heat to medium-low. Cook for 10 to 12 minutes or until eggs are set. Remove from heat, sprinkle with cheese and cover until cheese is melted.

Cheesy Vegetable Frittata

Ingredients

3 T. vegetable oil
1½ C. chopped zucchini
1½ C. chopped fresh mushrooms
¾ C. chopped onion
¾ C. chopped green bell pepper
1 clove garlic, minced
9 eggs
¼ C. half and half cream
2 (8 oz.) pkgs. cream cheese, cubed
2 C. shredded Cheddar cheese
4 slices whole wheat bread, cubed
1 tsp. salt
¼ tsp. pepper

Directions

Preheat oven to 350°. Heat oil in a large skillet over medium-high heat. Sauté zucchini, mushrooms, onion, bell pepper and garlic until tender; remove from heat. In a large bowl, beat together eggs and cream. Stir in cream cheese cubes, Cheddar cheese, bread cubes, vegetable mixture, salt and pepper. Mix well and pour into a greased 9 x 13″ baking dish. Bake for 1 hour or until eggs are set.

Confetti Frittata

Makes 6 servings

Ingredients

½ lb. (2 links) sweet Italian sausage, casings removed
1 T. olive oil or vegetable oil
1 red bell pepper, julienne-cut
1 green bell pepper, julienne-cut
1 yellow bell pepper, julienne-cut
1 large sweet onion, cut into 8 wedges
6 eggs
¾ C. milk
½ C. chopped fresh parsley
¼ tsp. chopped fresh rosemary
½ C. grated Parmesan cheese
½ tsp. salt
½ tsp. pepper

Directions

Preheat oven to 450°. In a large oven-proof skillet over medium-high heat, crumble and cook sausage until browned; drain grease. Transfer sausage to a bowl and set aside. Place oil in skillet then add bell peppers and onion. Sauté until the vegetables are tender and start to brown. Meanwhile, in a medium bowl, beat together eggs and milk; stir in parsley, rosemary, cheese, salt and pepper. When the vegetables are done, reduce heat to medium-low, add egg mixture and sprinkle sausage over all. As eggs cook, lift edges to allow uncooked eggs to flow underneath until all eggs are almost set, approximately 5 minutes. Place the skillet in the oven for 5 to 7 minutes or until the eggs are set. Let frittata stand a few minutes before serving.

Baked Potato, Apple & Ham Frittata

Makes 6 servings

Ingredients

3 C. frozen diced hash browns
    with onion and peppers, thawed
1 large red apple, cored and chopped
1 small onion, chopped
2 T. water
1 tsp. dried sage, crushed
1 C. diced ham
4 eggs
1½ C. milk
½ C. shredded Cheddar cheese
¼ tsp. salt

Directions

Preheat oven to 350°. Squeeze moisture from diced hash browns with paper towels; set aside. In a medium oven-proof skillet over medium-high heat, combine apple, onion, water and sage. Heat mixture until water boils then reduce heat to medium and cook until onion is translucent. Remove skillet from heat then stir in potatoes and ham. In a medium bowl, beat together eggs, milk, cheese and salt. Pour egg mixture into skillet but do not stir. Bake for 30 to 35 minutes or until eggs are set.

Waffles, Pancakes & French Toast

Buttermilk Pancakes

Makes 6 servings

Ingredients
3 C. all-purpose flour
3 T. sugar
3 tsp. baking powder
1½ tsp. baking soda
¾ tsp. salt
3 C. buttermilk
½ C. milk
3 eggs
⅓ C. butter or margarine, melted

Directions
In a large bowl, mix flour, sugar, baking powder,
baking soda and salt. In another large bowl, beat
together buttermilk, milk, eggs and melted butter.
Add the egg mixture to the flour mixture. Stir until
just blended, being careful not to over-mix the batter.
Pour approximately ⅓ to ½ cup of batter onto a greased
preheated griddle for each pancake. Once bubbles form
on the top of the pancakes, flip each to brown on the
other side.

Whole Wheat Pancakes

Makes 4 servings

Ingredients
1 C. whole wheat flour
⅔ C. all-purpose flour
⅓ C. wheat germ
1½ tsp. baking powder
½ tsp. baking soda
2 T. brown sugar
1 tsp. salt
5⅓ T. unsalted butter, softened
2½ C. buttermilk
2 eggs, beaten

Directions
In a large bowl, mix flours, wheat germ, baking powder, baking soda, brown sugar and salt. Cut the butter into the flour mixture until it has a sand-like consistency. Make a well in the center of the flour mixture and add the buttermilk and eggs. Stir until just blended, being careful not to over-mix the batter. Pour approximately ⅓ to ½ cup of batter onto a greased preheated griddle for each pancake. Once bubbles form on the top of the pancakes, flip each to brown on the other side.

27

Apple Pancakes

Ingredients

¼ C. butter or margarine, melted
1 egg
1 C. milk
1 C. shredded tart apple
1¼ C. all-purpose flour
1¼ tsp. baking powder
¼ tsp. cinnamon
1 T. sugar

Directions

In a large bowl, combine melted butter, egg, milk and apple. In a medium bowl, mix flour, baking powder, cinnamon and sugar. Add the flour mixture to the egg mixture. Stir until just blended, being careful not to over-mix the batter. Pour approximately ⅓ to ½ cup of batter onto a greased preheated griddle for each pancake. Once bubbles form on the top of the pancakes, flip each to brown on the other side.

Hearty Banana Oat Flapjacks

Makes 4 servings

Ingredients
2 large ripe bananas, peeled and sliced
1 T. sugar
1 C. all-purpose flour
½ C. quick or old-fashioned oats, uncooked
1 T. baking powder
¼ tsp. cinnamon
¼ tsp. salt (optional)
1 egg
1 C. milk
2 T. vegetable oil

Directions
In a medium bowl, stir banana slices with sugar until bananas are coated; set aside. In a large bowl, mix flour, oats, baking powder, cinnamon, and, if desired, salt. In a medium bowl, beat together egg, milk and oil. Add egg mixture to flour mixture. Stir until just blended, being careful not to over-mix the batter. Pour approximately ⅓ to ½ cup of batter onto a greased preheated griddle for each pancake. Top each pancake with four or five banana slices. Once bubbles form on the top of the pancakes, flip each to brown on the other side.

Pumpkin Pancakes

Makes 4 servings

Ingredients
2 C. all-purpose flour
3 T. brown sugar
2 tsp. baking powder
1 tsp. baking soda
1 tsp. cinnamon
½ tsp. ground ginger
1 tsp. ground allspice
½ tsp. salt
1½ C. milk
1 C. pumpkin puree
1 egg
2 T. vegetable oil
2 T. vinegar

Directions
In a large bowl, combine flour, brown sugar, baking powder, baking soda, cinnamon, ginger, allspice and salt. In a medium bowl, mix milk, pumpkin, egg, oil and vinegar. Add the egg mixture to the flour mixture. Stir until just blended, being careful not to over-mix the batter. Pour approximately ⅓ to ½ cup of batter onto a greased preheated griddle for each pancake. Once bubbles form on the top of the pancakes, flip each to brown on the other side.

Almond Pancakes & Orange Syrup

Makes 4 servings

Ingredients

½ C. whole wheat flour
½ C. all-purpose flour
4 tsp. sugar
¼ tsp. baking soda
¼ tsp. baking powder
⅛ tsp. salt
2 eggs, separated
¾ C. small-curd cottage cheese
⅔ C. milk
1 tsp. almond extract
2 T. canola oil
½ C. orange marmalade
½ C. maple syrup

Directions

In a large bowl, combine flours, sugar, soda, baking powder and salt. In a medium bowl, beat egg whites until stiff peaks form. In a medium bowl, combine egg yolks, cottage cheese, milk, almond extract and oil. Add the cottage cheese mixture to the flour mixture. Stir until just blended, then fold in the egg whites. Pour approximately ⅓ to ½ cup of batter onto a greased preheated griddle for each pancake. Once bubbles form on the top of the pancakes, flip each to brown on the other side. In a microwave-safe bowl, combine marmalade and syrup. Microwave for 15 seconds on high power, stir and serve warm with pancakes.

31

Old-Fashioned Pancakes

Makes 4 servings

Ingredients
1½ C. all-purpose flour
3½ tsp. baking powder
¾ tsp. salt
1 T. sugar
1 egg
1¼ C. milk
3 T. butter or margarine, melted
1 tsp. vanilla

Directions
In a large bowl, combine the flour, baking powder, salt and sugar. In a medium bowl, beat together egg, milk, melted butter and vanilla. Add the egg mixture to the flour mixture. Stir until just blended, being careful not to over-mix the batter. Pour approximately ⅓ to ½ cup of batter onto a greased preheated griddle for each pancake. Once bubbles form on the top of the pancakes, flip each to brown on the other side.

Blueberry Pancakes

Makes 4 servings

Ingredients

1 C. all-purpose flour
2 T. sugar
1¼ tsp. baking powder
¼ tsp. baking soda
¼ tsp. salt
½ tsp. orange zest
1 C. orange juice
2 T. milk
2 T. vegetable oil
1 egg
1 C. blueberries

Directions

In a large bowl, combine flour, sugar, baking powder, baking soda and salt. In a medium bowl, mix orange zest, juice, milk, oil and egg. Add orange mixture to flour mixture. Stir until just blended, being careful not to over-mix the batter. Pour approximately ⅓ to ½ cup of batter onto a greased preheated griddle for each pancake. Add a heaping tablespoon of blueberries to each pancake. Once bubbles form on the top of the pancakes, flip each to brown on the other side.

Fruit-Filled Baked Pancake

Makes 6 servings

Ingredients

1 T. butter or margarine
2 cooking apples, peeled, cored and thinly sliced
1 T. brown sugar
½ tsp. cinnamon
½ C. fresh raspberries, blueberries or other fresh berries
⅓ C. all-purpose flour
½ tsp. baking powder
⅛ tsp. salt
4 eggs, separated
⅓ C. sugar
⅓ C. milk
Powdered sugar

Directions

Preheat oven to 400°. Melt butter in a large oven-proof skillet over medium-high heat. Cook apple slices, brown sugar and cinnamon, stirring occasionally until apples are tender; mix in berries. Transfer fruit to a bowl; set aside. In a small bowl, mix flour, baking powder and salt. In a medium bowl, beat egg whites until soft peaks form. Add sugar, a little at a time, and continue beating until stiff peaks form. In a large bowl, beat egg yolks then alternately add flour mixture and milk. Gently fold in egg whites. Wipe clean and preheat the skillet in the hot oven for 10 minutes. Pour half of the batter into the greased skillet then spoon fruit mixture over batter. Pour remaining batter evenly over fruit. Bake for 20 to 25 minutes. Sprinkle with powdered sugar and cut into wedges to serve.

Easy Apple Blintz

Makes 4 servings

Ingredients
1 egg
¼ C. cottage cheese
1 C. whole milk
1 T. vegetable oil
¾ C. sour cream, divided
1 C. pancake mix
1 C. applesauce
Cinnamon (optional)

Directions
In a large bowl, mix egg, cottage cheese, milk, oil and ¼ cup sour cream. Add the pancake mix and stir until just blended, being careful not to over-mix the batter. Let the batter rest for 5 minutes. Pour approximately ⅓ to ½ cup of batter onto a greased preheated griddle for each pancake. Once bubbles form on the top of the pancakes, flip each to brown on the other side. To serve, spoon 1 tablespoon applesauce onto each pancake, fold in half and top each with a dollop of the remaining sour cream. If desired, sprinkle pancakes with cinnamon.

Light & Fluffy Pancakes

Makes 4 servings

Ingredients
1 C. all-purpose flour
1 T. sugar
2 tsp. baking powder
½ tsp. salt
1 egg
¾ C. milk
¼ C. shortening, melted

Directions
In a medium bowl, mix flour, sugar, baking powder and salt. In a small bowl, beat together egg, milk and shortening. Add egg mixture to flour mixture. Stir until just blended, being careful not to over-mix the batter. Pour approximately ⅓ to ½ cup of batter onto a greased preheated griddle for each pancake. Once bubbles form on the top of the pancakes, flip each to brown on the other side.

The Perfect Pancake Mix

Makes 7½ cups

Ingredients

4½ tsp. baking powder
3 tsp. baking soda
3 C. unbleached all-purpose flour
1½ tsp. salt
2 C. whole wheat or oat flour, or combination of both
1 C. cornmeal

Directions

In a large mixing bowl, sift baking powder, soda, all-purpose flour and salt. Mix in whole wheat or oat flours and cornmeal. Store in an air-tight container.

The Perfect Pancake Mix Pancakes
Makes 4 servings

2 eggs
1 C. milk
1 C. The Perfect Pancake Mix *(stir before each use)*

Directions

In a medium bowl, beat together eggs and milk. Add The Perfect Pancake Mix. Stir until just blended, being careful not to over-mix the batter. Pour approximately ⅓ to ½ cup of batter onto a greased preheated griddle for each pancake. Once bubbles form on the top of the pancakes, flip each to brown on the other side.

Potato Pancakes

Makes 6 servings

Ingredients

2 eggs
2 T. all-purpose flour
¼ tsp. baking powder
½ tsp. salt
¼ tsp. pepper
6 medium potatoes, peeled and shredded
½ C. finely chopped onion

Directions

In a large bowl, beat together eggs, flour, baking powder, salt and pepper. Stir in potatoes and onion. On a generously greased griddle or large skillet over medium heat, add a heaping tablespoon of the potato mixture for each pancake. Flatten each pancake with your spatula. Cook for approximately 3 minutes on each side until pancakes are browned and crisp. Place on paper towels to remove excess grease before serving.

Italian Potato Pancakes

Ingredients

½ tsp. onion powder
½ tsp. garlic powder
½ tsp. Italian seasoning
½ C. sour cream
½ medium red onion, diced
¼ C. chopped fresh parsley
½ C. Italian bread crumbs
2 eggs
1 tsp. salt
½ tsp. pepper
5 medium potatoes, peeled and shredded

Directions

In a small bowl, combine onion powder, garlic powder, Italian seasoning and sour cream; cover and refrigerate. In a large bowl, combine onion, parsley, bread crumbs, eggs, salt, pepper and shredded potatoes. On a generously greased griddle or large skillet over medium heat, add a heaping tablespoon of the potato mixture for each pancake. Flatten each pancake with your spatula. Cook for approximately 3 minutes on each side until pancakes are browned and crisp. Place on paper towels to remove excess grease before serving.

Sweet Potato Pancakes

Makes 4 servings

Ingredients
¾ lb. sweet potatoes
1½ C. all-purpose flour
3½ tsp. baking powder
1 tsp. salt
½ tsp. ground nutmeg
2 eggs
1½ C. milk
¼ C. butter or margarine, melted

Directions
In a medium pan of boiling water, cook sweet potatoes for approximately 15 minutes or until tender but firm. Drain water and immediately immerse potatoes in cold water to loosen skins. Drain, remove skins, chop and mash potatoes. In a large bowl, combine flour, baking powder, salt and nutmeg. In a medium bowl, beat together eggs, milk and butter then mix in sweet potatoes. Add potato mixture to flour mixture and stir until well combined. On a lightly greased griddle or large skillet over medium-high heat, add a heaping tablespoon of the potato mixture for each pancake. Flatten each pancake with your spatula. Cook on each side until pancakes are browned and crisp. Place on paper towels to remove excess grease before serving.

Sour Cream Waffles

Ingredients
2 C. flour
1½ tsp. baking soda
2 tsp. baking powder
2 tsp. salt
2 eggs
1 C. sour cream
1½ C. buttermilk

Directions
In a medium bowl, combine flour, baking soda, baking powder and salt. Add eggs, sour cream and buttermilk; beat until the batter is smooth. Pour ¼ to ⅓ cup batter onto a greased preheated waffle iron. Cook for approximately 3 to 4 minutes or until waffles are golden and fluffy.

Bacon Waffles

Makes 8 servings

Ingredients
1¾ C. all-purpose flour
1 T. sugar
2 tsp. baking powder
½ tsp. salt
3 eggs, separated
1½ C. milk
¼ C. butter or margarine, melted
1 lb. sliced bacon, cooked and crumbled

Directions
In a medium bowl, combine flour, sugar, baking powder and salt. In a small bowl, beat together egg yolks, milk and melted butter. Add egg mixture to flour mixture and stir until the batter is smooth. In a medium bowl, beat egg whites until stiff peaks form. Fold egg whites and bacon into batter. Pour ¼ to ⅓ cup batter onto a greased preheated waffle iron. Cook for approximately 3 to 4 minutes or until waffles are golden and fluffy.

Cinnamon Belgian Waffles

Makes 4 servings

Ingredients

2 eggs, separated
1 tsp. vanilla
1 C. buttermilk
¼ C. butter or margarine, melted
1 C. all-purpose flour
1½ tsp. baking powder
½ tsp. baking soda
½ T. sugar
¼ tsp. salt
1 pinch cinnamon

Directions

In a medium bowl, combine egg yolks, vanilla, buttermilk and butter. In a small bowl, mix flour, baking powder, baking soda, sugar, salt and cinnamon. Add flour mixture to buttermilk mixture and mix until batter is smooth. In a medium bowl, beat egg whites until stiff peaks form; fold into batter. Pour ¼ to ⅓ cup batter onto a greased preheated waffle iron. Cook for approximately 3 to 4 minutes or until waffles are golden and fluffy.

Classic Waffles

Ingredients

2 C. all-purpose flour
1 tsp. salt
4 tsp. baking powder
2 T. sugar
2 eggs
1½ C. warm milk
⅓ C. butter or margarine, melted
1 tsp. vanilla

Directions

In a large bowl, combine flour, salt, baking powder and sugar. In a medium bowl, beat together eggs, milk, butter and vanilla. Add egg mixture to flour mixture and mix until batter is smooth. Pour ¼ to ⅓ cup batter onto a greased preheated waffle iron. Cook for approximately 3 to 4 minutes or until waffles are golden and fluffy.

Belgian Waffles

Makes 6 servings

Ingredients
2 eggs, separated
5 T. sugar
1½ tsp. vanilla
½ C. butter or margarine, melted
1 tsp. salt
2¾ C. self-rising flour
2 C. warm milk

Directions
In a large bowl, beat egg yolks and sugar. Stir in vanilla, melted butter and salt. Alternately stir in flour and milk until batter is smooth. In a medium bowl, beat egg whites until stiff peaks form. Fold egg whites into batter. Let batter stand for 40 minutes. Pour ¼ to ⅓ cup batter onto a greased preheated waffle iron. Cook for approximately 3 to 4 minutes or until waffles are golden and fluffy.

Company French Toast Bake

Ingredients

¼ C. butter or margarine, softened
12 slices French bread (¾" each)
6 eggs
1½ C. milk
¼ C. sugar
2 T. maple syrup
1 T. vanilla
2 C. maple syrup
1 C. walnuts, chopped, toasted*
Powdered sugar

Directions

To prepare French toast, spread butter over bottom of a
9 x 13" baking dish. Place bread slices side by side in dish.
In a medium bowl, beat together eggs, milk, sugar, syrup
and vanilla. Pour egg mixture evenly over bread slices.
Flip each slice over to coat completely in egg mixture.
Cover dish and refrigerate for 8 to 12 hours. Preheat
oven to 450°. Uncover and bake for 13 to 15 minutes.
To prepare Walnut Syrup, in a medium pan over medium
heat, combine syrup and walnuts. Bring to a boil, reduce
heat to low and simmer for 8 to 10 minutes. Sprinkle
each serving of French toast with powdered sugar then
top with warm Walnut Syrup.

* To toast walnuts, bake at 350° for 8 to 10 minutes.

Make-Ahead Apple Cinnamon French Toast

Makes 8 servings

Ingredients

¾ C. butter or margarine, melted
1 C. brown sugar
1 tsp. cinnamon
2 (21 oz.) cans apple pie filling
20 slices white bread
6 eggs
1½ C. milk
1 tsp. vanilla
½ C. maple syrup

Directions

In a small bowl, combine butter, brown sugar and cinnamon. Spread the sugar mixture into the bottom of a greased 9 x 13″ baking dish. Spread pie filling evenly over brown sugar mixture. Press bread slices into filling, layering as necessary. In a medium bowl, beat together eggs, milk and vanilla. Evenly pour egg mixture over bread. Cover the pan with foil and refrigerate for 8 to 12 hours. Preheat oven to 350°. Bake covered dish for 75 minutes. Remove from oven, uncover and turn on broiler. Drizzle syrup over all and broil for 2 minutes or until the syrup begins to caramelize. Remove from oven, let stand for 10 minutes, cut into squares and invert pieces to serve.

47

Light & Yummy French Toast

Ingredients
¼ C. all-purpose flour
1 C. milk
1 pinch salt
3 eggs
½ tsp. cinnamon
1 tsp. vanilla
1 T. sugar
12 thick slices bread

Directions
In a large bowl, alternately add flour and milk while gently mixing. Mix in salt, eggs, cinnamon, vanilla and sugar until smooth. Dip bread slices in egg mixture until well-coated. Place each slice on a greased preheated griddle. Cook both sides over medium heat until golden brown.

Stuffed French Toast

Makes 6 servings

Ingredients
1 lb. loaf French bread
4 eggs
1 C. half and half cream
1½ tsp. vanilla, divided
½ tsp. ground nutmeg
1 (8 oz.) pkg. cream cheese, softened
2 T. sugar
½ tsp. cinnamon
½ C. chopped walnuts or pecans (optional)
1 C. apricot preserves
½ C. orange juice
½ tsp. almond extract

Directions
Cut bread into 10 to 12 slices, each approximately
1½" thick. Create a pocket in the middle of each piece
by cutting a small slice with your knife. In a shallow
bowl, beat together eggs, cream, ½ teaspoon vanilla and
nutmeg. In another small bowl, combine cream cheese,
sugar, 1 teaspoon vanilla, cinnamon and, if desired, nuts.
Fill each bread slice with a heaping tablespoon of the
cream cheese mixture. Dip each slice into the egg mixture
being sure to coat both sides. Place each slice on a greased
preheated griddle. Cook both sides until golden brown.
In a small bowl, combine preserves, juice and almond
extract. To serve, drizzle French toast with glaze.

49

Baked French Toast

Ingredients
1 (1 lb.) loaf French bread
8 eggs
2 C. milk
1½ C. half and half cream
2 tsp. vanilla
¼ tsp. cinnamon
¾ C. butter or margarine
1⅓ C. brown sugar
3 T. light corn syrup

Directions
Cut bread diagonally into approximately 1″ slices.
Arrange slices in the bottom of a greased 9 x 13″ baking
dish. In a large bowl, beat together eggs, milk, cream,
vanilla and cinnamon. Pour evenly over bread slices; cover
and refrigerate for 8 to 12 hours. Preheat oven to 350°.
In a small pan over medium-high heat, mix butter, brown
sugar and corn syrup. Cook, stirring often, until bubbly.
Pour over egg mixture. Bake, uncovered, for 40 minutes.

Peach French Toast

Ingredients
2 T. butter or margarine
2 T. brown sugar
2 ripe peaches, cut into ½" slices
2 T. plus ¾ C. heavy cream, divided
8 slices white, sourdough or brioche bread
3 eggs
⅛ tsp. cinnamon
Powdered sugar

Directions
Melt butter in a large skillet over medium-low heat.
Sprinkle brown sugar over butter and stir. Increase heat to
medium-high, add peach slices and cook, stirring often,
for 3 minutes. Stir in 2 tablespoons of cream and simmer
for 2 minutes. Transfer peach mixture to a bowl. In a
medium bowl, beat ¾ cup cream until stiff peaks form.
Place in refrigerator until ready to serve. Divide peach
mixture evenly on four slices of bread then top with
the other four slices. In a shallow bowl, beat together
eggs and cinnamon. Soak each side of each sandwich
in the egg mixture for 30 seconds. Place each sandwich
on a greased preheated griddle. Cook both sides until
golden brown. Cut sandwiches in half, sprinkle each with
powdered sugar and serve with whipped cream.

French Toast Waffles

Makes 2 to 3 servings

Ingredients
1 egg
2 T. butter or margarine, melted
½ C. milk
⅛ tsp. salt
⅛ tsp. ground nutmeg
½ tsp. vanilla
4 to 6 bread slices, your choice, crust removed if preferred

Directions
In a shallow bowl or plate, beat together egg, melted butter, milk, salt, nutmeg and vanilla. Dip each side of each bread slice into the egg mixture, coating well, but not soaking. Cook the bread slices in a well-greased preheated waffle iron until crisp.

Blueberry French Toast Bake

Makes 12 servings

Ingredients

1 (1 lb.) loaf Italian bread, cut into 1" cubes, divided
1 tsp. cinnamon, divided
1 (8 oz.) pkg. cream cheese, diced in ½" cubes
1 C. blueberries
10 eggs
2 C. milk
1 tsp. vanilla
⅓ C. maple syrup
Maple syrup

Directions

In a greased 9 x 13" baking dish, spread half of the bread cubes. Sprinkle ½ teaspoon cinnamon over bread cubes and toss. Place cream cheese cubes over bread then top with blueberries and remaining bread cubes. Sprinkle ½ teaspoon cinnamon over top of all, tossing top bread cubes to coat with cinnamon. In a large bowl, beat together eggs, milk, vanilla and maple syrup. Pour egg mixture evenly over bread cubes. Cover dish with foil and refrigerate for 8 to 12 hours. Remove pan from refrigerator and allow to sit for 30 minutes before baking. Preheat oven to 350°. Bake covered dish for 30 minutes. Uncover and continue to bake for an additional 30 minutes until golden brown and center is set. Serve casserole with maple syrup.

53

Berry Yummy French Toast

Ingredients
2 C. frozen blueberries
1½ C. frozen blackberries
1½ C. frozen raspberries
½ C. plus 1 T. sugar, divided
1 T. cornstarch
1 tsp. cinnamon
1 C. milk
1 tsp. vanilla
4 egg whites
1 egg
1 (8 oz.) loaf French bread, cut into 1" slices
Powdered sugar

Directions
Preheat oven to 350°. In a greased 9 x 13" baking dish, combine blueberries, blackberries, raspberries, ½ cup sugar, cornstarch and cinnamon. In a shallow bowl, beat together milk, vanilla, egg whites and egg. Soak each side of each bread slice in mixture before arranging slices in an even layer over berries. Sprinkle bread with 1 tablespoon sugar. Bake for 30 minutes or until golden brown. To serve, sprinkle each slice with powdered sugar.

Quiches

Ham & Swiss Quiche

Ingredients

4 eggs
1 C. half and half cream
1 T. Dijon mustard
⅛ tsp. white pepper
1 (9″) unbaked pie crust
1½ C. cubed ham
1½ C. shredded Swiss cheese
1 C. frozen chopped spinach or frozen broccoli
    florets, thawed and well drained
2 T. grated Parmesan cheese

Directions

Preheat oven to 350°. In a medium bowl, beat together eggs, cream, mustard and white pepper. In pie crust, layer ham, Swiss cheese and the vegetable of your choice. Pour egg mixture over all and sprinkle with Parmesan cheese. Place pie plate on a baking sheet and bake for 40 to 50 minutes or until center is set. Let stand for 10 minutes before serving.

Tomato & Basil Quiche

Makes 4 servings

Ingredients
1 (9") unbaked deep-dish pie crust
1 T. olive oil
1 onion, sliced
2 T. all-purpose flour
2 tsp. dried basil
2 tomatoes, peeled and sliced
3 eggs
½ C. milk
Salt and pepper to taste
1½ C. shredded Colby-Monterey Jack cheese, divided

Directions
Preheat oven to 400°. Prick pie crust with a fork then bake for 8 minutes. Meanwhile, heat olive oil in a large skillet over medium heat. Sauté onion until translucent. Transfer onion to a bowl; set aside. In a shallow bowl, combine flour and basil. Toss tomato slices in flour mixture then add to skillet and sauté for 1 minute on each side. In a small bowl, beat together eggs and milk. Season with salt and pepper. In baked pie crust, spread 1 cup cheese over bottom then layer onion, tomatoes and egg mixture. Sprinkle remaining ½ cup cheese over egg mixture. Place pie plate on a baking sheet and bake for 10 minutes. Reduce oven temperature to 350° and bake for an additional 15 to 20 minutes or until center is set. Let stand for 10 minutes before serving.

Bacon Quiche Tarts

Ingredients
5 slices bacon
1 (8 oz.) pkg. cream cheese, softened
2 T. milk
2 eggs
½ C. shredded Swiss cheese
2 T. chopped green onion
1 (10 oz.) can refrigerated flaky biscuit dough

Directions
Preheat oven to 375°. Lightly grease 10 muffin cups. In
a large skillet over medium-high heat, cook bacon until
crisp. Drain, crumble and set aside. In a medium bowl,
beat cream cheese, milk and eggs on low speed until
smooth. Stir in cheese and onion. Press 1 biscuit into
the bottom and up the sides of each greased muffin cup.
Sprinkle half of the crumbled bacon into the biscuit cups
then spoon 2 tablespoons of the cream cheese mixture into
each cup. Bake for 20 to 25 minutes or until filling is set.
Sprinkle the remaining bacon onto tarts and serve warm.

Asparagus Quiche

Makes 12 servings

Ingredients

1 lb. fresh asparagus, trimmed and cut into ½″ pieces
10 slices bacon
2 C. shredded Swiss cheese
2 (8″) unbaked pie crusts
4 eggs
1½ C. half and half cream
¼ tsp. ground nutmeg
Salt and pepper to taste

Directions

Preheat oven to 400°. In a covered double boiler, steam asparagus over 1″ of water. Cook until tender but firm; drain and set aside. In a large skillet over medium-high heat, cook bacon until crisp; drain, crumble and set aside. Sprinkle bacon and cheese evenly into pie crusts. In a medium bowl, beat together eggs, cream and nutmeg. Season with salt and pepper. Pour egg mixture over bacon and cheese. Place pie plates on a baking sheet and bake for 35 to 40 minutes or until center is set. Let stand for 10 minutes before serving.

Cajun Quiche

Makes 12 servings

Ingredients

2 (9″) unbaked deep-dish pie crusts
6 eggs
1½ C. shredded American cheese
½ C. shredded Monterey Jack cheese
1 bunch green onions, chopped
2 C. heavy or whipping cream
1 tsp. Creole seasoning
½ lb. medium shrimp, shelled and deveined
1 lb. fresh lump or jumbo crabmeat
    or 1 (16 oz.) can refrigerated, pasteurized
    crabmeat, picked over and flaked

Directions

Preheat oven to 350°. Prick the bottoms of each crust
with a fork. Bake for 10 to 12 minutes until golden
brown. In a large bowl, beat eggs then add cheeses,
onions, cream and Creole seasoning. Fold in shrimp then
gently fold in crabmeat. Spoon filling into pie crusts.
Place pie plates on a baking sheet and bake for 50 to 55
minutes or until center is set. Let stand for 10 minutes
before serving.

Crab & Swiss Quiche

Ingredients
2 eggs
½ C. milk
½ C. mayonnaise
1 tsp. cornstarch
½ lb. fresh lump or imitation crabmeat, flaked
1½ C. shredded Swiss cheese
1 (9″) unbaked pie crust

Directions
Preheat oven to 350°. In a medium bowl, beat together eggs, milk, mayonnaise and cornstarch. Stir in crab and cheese until well combined. Pour mixture into pie crust. Place pie plate on a baking sheet and bake for 30 to 40 minutes or until center is set. Let stand for 10 minutes before serving.

Pizza Quiche

Ingredients
1 (9") unbaked pie crust
2 C. shredded mozzarella cheese
1 C. shredded Cheddar cheese
1 C. shredded Monterey Jack cheese
¾ C. pepperoni slices
1 (4.5 oz.) jar sliced mushrooms, well drained
1 T. olive oil
½ C. finely chopped onion
2 cloves garlic, minced
3 eggs
1 C. whole milk
1 tsp. dried Italian seasoning

Directions
Preheat oven to 400°. Spread cheeses over bottom of
unbaked pie crust. Layer pepperoni and mushrooms
over cheeses. Heat olive oil in a small skillet over
medium-high heat. Sauté onion and garlic until onion
is translucent; sprinkle over all. In a medium bowl, beat
together eggs, milk and Italian seasoning; pour into pie
crusts. Place pie plate on a baking sheet and bake for
40 to 45 minutes or until center is set. Let stand for 10
minutes before serving.

Crustless Spinach Quiche

Makes 4 servings

Ingredients
1 T. vegetable oil
1 onion, chopped
1 tsp. minced garlic
1 (10 oz.) pkg. frozen chopped spinach,
    thawed and well-drained
5 eggs
3 C. shredded Muenster cheese
¼ tsp. salt
⅛ tsp. pepper

Directions
Preheat oven to 350°. Heat oil in a large skillet over medium-high heat. Sauté onion and garlic until onion is translucent. Stir in spinach and continue cooking until any excess moisture is gone. In a large bowl, beat eggs then stir in cheese, salt and pepper. Add spinach mixture to eggs and mix until well combined. Pour mixture into a lightly greased 9″ pie plate. Place pie plate on a baking sheet and bake for 30 minutes or until center is set. Let stand for 10 minutes before serving.

Easy One-Bowl Quiche

Ingredients

2 C. milk

4 eggs

¾ C. biscuit baking mix

¼ C. butter or margarine, softened

1 C. grated Parmesan cheese

1 (10 oz.) pkg. chopped frozen broccoli,
    thawed and well-drained

1 C. cubed ham

2 C. shredded Cheddar cheese

Directions

Preheat oven to 375°. In a large bowl, beat together milk, eggs, baking mix, butter and Parmesan cheese until well combined but still lumpy. Stir in broccoli, ham and Cheddar cheese. Pour into a lightly greased 10″ pie plate. Place pie plate on a baking sheet and bake for 50 minutes or until center is set. Let stand for 10 minutes before serving.

Easy Tortilla Quiche

Makes 8 servings

Ingredients

¾ lb. bulk pork sausage
5 (6") corn tortillas
1 C. shredded Monterey Jack cheese
1 C. shredded Cheddar cheese
¼ C. canned chopped green chiles, drained
6 eggs
½ C. whipping cream
½ C. small curd cottage cheese
½ tsp. chili powder
¼ C. minced fresh cilantro or parsley

Directions

Preheat oven to 350°. In a large skillet over medium-high heat, crumble and cook sausage until no longer brown; drain grease. Place 4 tortillas around the outside of a 9" pie plate, overlapping and extending the tortillas ½" beyond plate rim. Place remaining tortilla in the center. Layer cooked sausage, cheeses and chiles over tortillas. In a medium bowl, beat together eggs, cream, cottage cheese and chili powder; pour into pie plate. Place pie plate on a baking sheet and bake for 45 minutes or until center is set. Sprinkle with cilantro. Let stand for 10 minutes before serving.

Classic Quiche

Makes 16 servings

Ingredients

1 (10 oz.) pkg. frozen chopped spinach, thawed
2 T. olive oil
1 onion, finely diced
½ lb. fresh mushrooms, finely diced
2 C. finely diced smoked ham
½ lb. thick sliced bacon, cooked and crumbled
1 (8 oz.) container sour cream
Salt and pepper to taste
2 (9″) unbaked deep-dish pie crusts
2 C. shredded Monterey Jack cheese
2 C. shredded Cheddar cheese
1 C. grated Parmesan cheese
8 eggs
1½ C. half and half cream
1 T. dried parsley

Directions

Preheat oven to 375°. Cook spinach according to
package instructions, cool and squeeze dry. Heat oil in
a large skillet over medium-high heat. Sauté onion until
translucent. Stir in mushrooms and sauté for 2 minutes.
Stir in ham and bacon, remove skillet from heat and
set aside. In a large bowl, mix spinach and sour cream.
Season with salt and pepper. Pour spinach mixture into
unbaked pie crusts. Spread ham mixture over spinach
mixture. Combine cheeses and spread over ham mixture.
In a medium bowl, beat together eggs, cream and parsley,
then pour into pies. Place pie plates on a baking sheet
and bake for 40 minutes or until centers are set.

Ham & Swiss Puff-Pastry Quiche

Makes 8 servings

Ingredients
1 (17.3 oz.) pkg. frozen puff pastry (2 sheets), thawed
1 C. diced ham
2 C. shredded Swiss cheese
2 C. sliced mushrooms
2 eggs
1 T. chopped fresh rosemary
½ tsp. pepper
½ tsp. salt
¼ tsp. ground nutmeg
1 C. sour cream

Directions
Preheat oven to 400°. Unfold each pastry sheet onto separate baking sheets. Top each pastry evenly with ham, cheese and mushrooms to within ½″ of the edge of the pastry. In a small bowl, beat together eggs, rosemary, pepper, salt and nutmeg; stir in sour cream. Spread sour cream mixture over toppings on each pastry. Bake for 25 minutes or until pastries are puffed and eggs are set.

Huevos Rancheros

Ingredients

½ tsp. ground cumin
1 (16 oz.) can black beans, rinsed and drained
1 chipotle chili in adobo sauce, diced
    or ½ tsp. crushed red pepper flakes (optional)
4 (6 to 8″) corn tortillas
½ C. salsa
4 eggs, fried
⅔ C. shredded Monterey Jack cheese
1 ripe avocado, peeled and sliced

Directions

Preheat oven to 425°. In a small pan over medium heat, toast cumin for approximately 3 minutes or until it becomes fragrant. Add beans and, if desired, chipotle until warmed. Warm tortillas then layer some of the bean mixture, salsa, 1 fried egg and cheese onto each tortilla. Bake until cheese is melted. Serve with avocado slices.

Sandwiches & Wraps

Breakfast Bruschetta

Makes 4 servings

Ingredients
1 large tomato, seeded and chopped
2 green onions, thinly sliced
1 tsp. finely chopped fresh basil
1 tsp. Dijon mustard
4 eggs
¼ C. milk
⅛ tsp. salt
1 dash pepper
4 (¾″ thick) slices French or Italian bread
1 T. butter or margarine
¼ C. diced ham

Directions
In a small bowl, combine chopped tomato, green onions, basil and mustard. In a medium bowl, beat together eggs, milk, salt and pepper; set aside. In a large skillet over medium heat, toast bread slices on both sides; set aside. Melt butter in skillet then add egg mixture. As eggs cook, lift edges to allow uncooked eggs to flow underneath until all eggs are almost set. Sprinkle ham over eggs and continue to cook until eggs are set. Divide the egg mixture into fourths. To serve, top each toast slice with eggs then tomato mixture.

Italian Breakfast Burrito

Makes 6 servings

Ingredients

2 T. olive oil
2 C. chopped fresh baby spinach
½ C. chopped prosciutto
½ C. chopped fresh basil
1 (6 oz.) jar marinated artichoke hearts, drained
3 shallots, finely chopped
2 cloves garlic, minced
8 eggs
Salt and pepper to taste
6 (10″) flour tortillas
½ C. prepared basil pesto
1½ C. shredded mozzarella cheese
1 (15 oz.) container marinara sauce, warmed

Directions

Heat olive oil in a large skillet over medium heat. Add spinach, prosciutto, basil, artichoke hearts, shallots and garlic. Cook, stirring often, until spinach wilts. In a medium bowl, beat eggs. Season with salt and pepper. Pour eggs over vegetable mixture in skillet. Continue cooking over medium heat. As eggs cook, lift edges to allow uncooked eggs to flow underneath until all eggs are set. Divide eggs into 6 portions. Warm tortillas then spread pesto over tortillas, leaving 1″ around edge. Sprinkle cheese over pesto and place eggs over cheese. Roll tortillas into wraps and serve with marinara sauce.

Caramelized Onion, Canadian Bacon, & Egg Sandwiches

Makes 4 servings

Ingredients

2 tsp. canola oil
2½ C. thinly vertically sliced onions
½ tsp. sugar
½ tsp. tarragon vinegar
¼ tsp. salt
¼ tsp. pepper
4 slices Canadian bacon
4 eggs
8 slices white bread, toasted

Directions

Heat oil in a large skillet over medium-high heat. Sauté onions, sugar, vinegar, salt and pepper until onions are golden. Remove onion mixture and set aside. Add Canadian bacon to pan and cook each side until lightly browned. Remove Canadian bacon and set aside. Wipe out skillet then lightly grease. Reduce heat to medium and add eggs, one at a time, to pan. Fry each egg on both sides until cooked to desired doneness. Layer 1 Canadian bacon slice, ¼ cup onion mixture and 1 egg on 4 toast slices. Top sandwiches with remaining 4 toast slices.

72

Prosciutto & Egg Panini

Makes 4 servings

Ingredients
8 eggs
½ tsp. salt
¼ tsp. pepper
2 T. butter or margarine, divided
4 soft rolls, halved lengthwise
8 oz. prosciutto, thinly sliced
1 C. Swiss cheese, thinly sliced

Directions
In a medium bowl, beat together eggs, salt and pepper. Melt 1 tablespoon butter in a large skillet over medium heat. Add egg mixture and cook, stirring often to scramble, until eggs are cooked through. Divide the eggs onto the bottom of the 4 rolls and top with prosciutto, cheese and the tops of the rolls. Melt the remaining 1 tablespoon of butter in a large skillet over medium heat. Place sandwiches in skillet. Cook, pressing frequently with the spatula, until cheese has melted and the rolls are golden brown.

Egg & Ham Pitas

Ingredients
3 eggs
3 egg whites
½ C. finely diced ham
3 T. water
2 T. thinly sliced chives
⅛ tsp. salt
2 T. light cream cheese, diced
2 (6 or 7") pita breads, warmed

Directions
In a medium bowl, beat together eggs, egg whites, ham, water, chives and salt. In a lightly greased large skillet over medium heat, add egg mixture. Place diced cream cheese cubes over eggs and cook, stirring often to scramble, until eggs are cooked through. Warm pitas then cut in half. Fill each half with some of the egg mixture.

Breakfast Pita Pockets

Makes 4 servings

Ingredients
4 slices bacon
4 links sausage
4 slices Canadian bacon
Sliced vegetables (optional)
6 eggs, beaten
2 pita breads, cut in half
4 slices American cheese

Directions
In a medium skillet over medium heat, cook bacon, sausage and Canadian bacon. Drain grease, crumble bacon and chop sausage links; set aside. If desired, sauté vegetables in skillet until tender; set aside. Add beaten eggs to skillet and cook over medium heat, stirring often to scramble, until eggs are almost cooked through. Add meat and vegetable mixtures and continue to heat until eggs are cooked through. Warm pitas and place 1 slice of cheese into each half. Divide egg mixture between each pita half.

Breakfast Burritos

Makes 4 servings

Ingredients
½ lb. bulk pork sausage
1 large potato, peeled and grated
4 eggs
4 (8 to 10") flour tortillas
1 large tomato, diced
1 C. shredded mozzarella cheese
    or shredded Cheddar cheese
Salsa (optional)

Directions
In a medium skillet over medium-high heat, crumble and cook sausage until browned. Add grated potato and cook until golden. Drain grease and set aside. Reduce heat to medium, add eggs and cook, stirring often to scramble, until eggs are cooked through. Warm tortillas and divide sausage and potato mixture, eggs, diced tomato and cheese evenly between the 4 tortillas. Roll tortillas into wraps and serve with salsa, if desired.

South of the Border Breakfast Tacos

Makes 4 servings

Ingredients
1 T. butter or margarine
1 C. diced cooked potato cubes
4 eggs, beaten
4 slices bacon, cooked and crumbled
4 (8 to 10") flour tortillas
¾ C. shredded Cheddar cheese
½ C. picante sauce

Directions
Melt butter in a medium skillet over medium-high heat. Add potato cubes and cook until lightly browned. Add beaten eggs and bacon to skillet. Cook, stirring often to scramble eggs, until eggs are cooked through. Warm tortillas. Divide egg mixture, cheese and picante sauce between the 4 tortillas. Roll tortillas into wraps and serve.

Bacon Chive Croissants

Ingredients
4 eggs, beaten
4 medium croissants, split, lightly toasted
4 T. chive and onion cream cheese spread
¼ tsp. pepper
12 slices bacon, cooked

Directions
In a medium skillet over medium heat, cook eggs, stirring often to scramble, until eggs are cooked through. Spread insides of croissants with cream cheese spread. Divide egg mixture evenly onto croissant bottoms. Sprinkle eggs with pepper then add three cooked bacon slices to each. Cover with croissant tops and serve.

Fried Egg Sandwiches

Makes 4 servings

Ingredients

2 tsp. butter or margarine
4 eggs
Salt and pepper to taste
4 slices American cheese
8 slices white bread, toasted
2 T. mayonnaise
2 T. ketchup

Directions

Melt butter in a medium skillet over medium-high heat.
Add eggs to pan, one at a time, frying on each side to
desired doneness. Season with salt and pepper. Place a
slice of cheese over each egg. Once cheese melts, divide
eggs onto 4 slices of toast. Spread mayonnaise and
ketchup on remaining toast slices then place on top of
eggs to create sandwiches.

Spicy Mexican Breakfast Tacos

Ingredients

6 oz. chorizo sausage
6 eggs
¼ C. milk
½ tsp. salt
½ tsp. pepper
8 (6″) corn tortillas
1 C. shredded Monterey Jack cheese
4 dashes hot pepper sauce or to taste
½ C. salsa

Directions

In a large skillet over medium-high heat, crumble sausage and cook until browned; drain grease. Transfer sausage to a bowl and set aside. In a medium bowl, beat together eggs, milk, salt and pepper. Reduce heat to medium and add egg mixture. Cook, stirring often to scramble, until eggs are almost set. Add sausage and continue to cook eggs until heated through. In a large skillet over medium-high heat, warm tortillas until they are crispy on the edges but pliable. Sprinkle cheese over each tortilla, top with egg and sausage mixture then add a dash of hot pepper sauce and salsa to each. Roll tortillas into wraps and serve.

Bacon Breakfast Burritos

Makes 10 servings

Ingredients
1 lb. sliced bacon
10 eggs
1 (16 oz.) can refried beans
10 (10″) flour tortillas
2 C. shredded Cheddar cheese

Directions
In a large skillet over medium-high heat, cook bacon until crisp; drain, transfer to a plate and set aside. Add eggs to skillet, one at a time, and fry each side until cooked to desired doneness. In a small pan over medium heat, warm refried beans. Top each tortilla with refried beans, cheese, 2 strips of bacon and 1 fried egg. Roll tortillas into wraps and serve.

Bacon-Potato Burritos

Makes 4 servings

Ingredients
8 slices bacon
1½ C. frozen Southern-style hash browns
2 tsp. dried minced onion
4 eggs
¼ C. milk
1 tsp. Worcestershire sauce
¼ tsp. salt
¼ tsp. pepper
1 C. shredded Cheddar cheese
6 (8") flour tortillas

Directions
In a large skillet over medium-high heat, cook bacon until crisp; drain, crumble and set aside. Add hash browns and onion to skillet, stirring often. In a medium bowl, beat together eggs, milk, Worcestershire sauce, salt and pepper. Pour over potatoes and cook, stirring often, until eggs are cooked through. Stir in crumbled bacon. Sprinkle egg mixture with cheese. Warm tortillas then divide egg mixture evenly between each tortilla. Roll tortillas into wraps and serve.

French Toast Bacon Sandwich

Ingredients

8 eggs, divided
8 slices bread
8 slices bacon
½ C. maple syrup

Directions

In a shallow bowl, beat 4 eggs. Dip both sides of each bread slice in egg mixture then cook on a lightly greased griddle over medium-high heat until browned on each side. Transfer French toast to a plate and cover to keep warm. Place bacon in skillet and cook until crisp; drain grease and set aside. Reduce heat to medium and add remaining 4 eggs, one a time, frying each side until cooked to desired doneness. To serve, place 1 egg and 2 strips of bacon on 4 slices of French toast. Top with remaining slices of French toast then drizzle syrup on each sandwich.

Ham & Swiss Rolls

Makes 4 servings

Ingredients
1 (8 oz.) pkg. refrigerated crescent rolls
1 C. diced ham
¾ C. shredded Swiss cheese
1½ tsp. mustard
1 T. finely chopped onion

Directions
Preheat oven to 375°. Separate crescent rolls into eight triangles. In a medium bowl, combine ham, cheese, mustard and onion. Place 2 tablespoons ham mixture in the center of each triangle. Fold dough points towards centers and pinch edges to seal dough. Place rolls on a lightly greased baking sheet. Bake for 11 to 13 minutes or until rolls are golden brown.

Casseroles

Easy Country Breakfast Casserole

Makes 8 servings

Ingredients

1 lb. bulk pork sausage
6 eggs
2 C. milk
1 tsp. salt
1 tsp. dry mustard
6 slices white bread, cut into ½" cubes
1 C. shredded Cheddar cheese

Directions

In a large skillet over medium-high heat, crumble and cook sausage until browned; drain grease and set aside. In a large bowl, beat together eggs, milk, salt and dry mustard. Stir in bread cubes, cheese and cooked sausage. Pour mixture into a greased 7 x 11" baking dish. Cover and refrigerate for 8 to 12 hours. Remove dish from refrigerator and let stand for 30 minutes. Preheat oven to 350°. Bake, uncovered, for 40 minutes or until center is set. Let stand 10 minutes before serving.

Cheesy Asparagus Strata

Makes 10 servings

Ingredients

1½ lbs. fresh asparagus, cut into 2" pieces
3 T. butter or margarine, melted
1 (1 lb.) loaf sliced bread, crusts removed
¾ C. shredded Cheddar cheese, divided
2 C. cubed ham
6 eggs
3 C. milk
2 tsp. dried minced onion
½ tsp. salt
¼ tsp. dry mustard

Directions

In a medium saucepan filled with boiling water, cook asparagus until tender but firm; drain and set aside. Brush 1 side of each slice of bread with butter. Place half of the bread slices in a single layer, buttered side up, in a greased 9 x 13" baking dish. Layer ½ cup cheese, asparagus, ham and remaining bread slices, buttered side up. In a medium bowl, beat together eggs, milk, onion, salt and dry mustard. Pour over bread, cover dish and refrigerate for 8 to 12 hours. Preheat oven to 325°. Bake, uncovered, for 50 minutes. Sprinkle with remaining ¼ cup cheese and bake for an additional 5 to 10 minutes or until eggs are set and cheese is melted. Let stand 10 minutes before serving.

Ham & Asparagus Egg Bake

Makes 12 servings

Ingredients

1½ C. chopped ham
½ C. chopped onion
¼ C. chopped red bell pepper
1 (10 oz.) pkg. frozen cut asparagus, thawed
8 eggs
2 C. milk
1 C. all-purpose flour
¼ C. grated Parmesan cheese
¾ tsp. dried tarragon
¾ tsp. salt
½ tsp. pepper
1 C. shredded Cheddar cheese

Directions

Preheat oven to 425°. In a greased 9 x 13″ baking dish, combine ham, onion, bell pepper and asparagus. In a large bowl, beat together eggs, milk, flour, Parmesan cheese, tarragon, salt and pepper. Pour egg mixture over ham mixture in baking dish. Bake for 20 minutes or until center is set. Sprinkle with Cheddar cheese and bake for an additional 5 minutes or until cheese is melted. Let stand 10 minutes before serving.

Zucchini Egg Bake

Makes 6 servings

Ingredients
¼ C. butter or margarine
3 C. peeled, chopped zucchini
1 large onion, chopped
2 garlic cloves, minced
4 eggs
½ C. grated Parmesan cheese
¼ C. chopped fresh parsley
1½ tsp. chopped fresh basil
1½ tsp. chopped fresh marjoram
½ tsp. salt
½ C. shredded Monterey Jack cheese

Directions
Preheat oven to 350°. Melt butter in a large skillet over medium-high heat. Sauté zucchini, onion and garlic until tender; set aside. In a large bowl, beat together eggs, Parmesan cheese, parsley, basil, marjoram and salt. Stir in zucchini mixture and Monterey Jack cheese. Pour into a greased 1-quart baking dish. Bake for 20 to 25 minutes or until center is set. Let stand for 10 minutes before serving.

Apple-Raisin French Toast Strata

Makes 12 servings

Ingredients
1 (1 lb.) loaf cinnamon-raisin bread, cubed
1 (8 oz.) pkg. cream cheese, cubed
1 C. diced peeled apples
8 eggs
2½ C. half and half cream
6 T. butter or margarine, melted
¼ C. maple syrup

Directions
In a greased 9 x 13″ baking dish, arrange half of the bread cubes. Layer cream cheese cubes and diced apples over bread cubes. Top with remaining bread cubes. In a large bowl, beat together eggs, cream, melted butter and maple syrup; pour over bread mixture. Using a spoon or fork, press down on the top layer of bread cubes to ensure all bread pieces soak in egg mixture. Cover dish and refrigerate for 2 to 6 hours. Preheat oven to 325°. Bake for 45 minutes. Let stand for 10 minutes before serving.

Simple Crescent Crust Egg Bake

Makes 12 servings

Ingredients
1 lb. bulk pork sausage
1 (8 oz.) pkg. refrigerated crescent roll dough
8 eggs
2 C. shredded mozzarella cheese
2 C. shredded Cheddar cheese
1 tsp. dried oregano

Directions
In a large skillet over medium-high heat, crumble and cook sausage until browned; drain. Preheat oven to 350°. Line the bottom of a greased 9 x 13″ baking dish with crescent roll dough then spread sausage over dough. In a large bowl, beat together eggs, cheeses and oregano. Pour egg mixture over sausage. Bake for 25 to 30 minutes or until center is set. Let stand for 10 minutes before serving.

Egg Enchiladas

Makes 10 servings

Ingredients

1 lb. chopped ham
¾ C. sliced green onion
¾ C. chopped green bell pepper
3 C. shredded Cheddar cheese, divided
10 (8") flour tortillas
5 eggs, beaten
2 C. half and half cream
½ C. milk
1 T. all-purpose flour
¼ tsp. garlic powder
1 dash hot pepper sauce
Salsa
Sour cream

Directions

In a food processor, pulse ham until finely ground. In a large bowl, combine ham, onion and bell pepper. Spread ⅓ cup ham mixture and 3 tablespoons cheese onto each tortilla. Roll each tortilla and place, seam side down, in a greased 9 x 13" baking dish. In a medium bowl, beat together eggs, cream, milk, flour, garlic powder and hot pepper sauce. Pour egg mixture over tortillas, ensuring egg mixture almost completely covers tortillas. Cover dish and refrigerate for 8 to 12 hours. Preheat oven to 350°. Bake, uncovered, for 50 to 60 minutes or until eggs are set. Sprinkle with remaining 1 cup cheese and bake for an additional 5 minutes. Let stand for 10 minutes before serving with salsa and sour cream.

Southwest Breakfast Lasagna

Makes 6 to 8 servings

Ingredients

1 lb. bulk pork sausage
1 small onion, chopped
½ green bell pepper, chopped
2 (10 oz.) cans diced tomatoes and green chiles
8 (10") flour tortillas, torn into bite-size pieces
3 C. shredded Colby-Monterey Jack cheese
6 eggs
2 C. milk
1 tsp. salt
½ tsp. pepper

Directions

Preheat oven to 350°. In a large skillet over medium-high heat, crumble and cook sausage until browned. Drain grease and add onion and bell pepper. Sauté over medium-high heat for 5 minutes or until vegetables are tender. Stir in tomatoes and chiles, reduce heat to medium-low and simmer for 10 minutes. In a greased 9 x 13" baking dish, layer half of the tortilla pieces, half of the sausage mixture and half of the cheese. Repeat layers. In a medium bowl, beat together eggs, milk, salt and pepper; pour over cheese. Bake, lightly covered, for 30 minutes or until center is set. Let stand for 10 minutes before serving.

Baked Omelet Casserole

Makes 8 servings

Ingredients

¼ C. butter or margarine
1 small onion, chopped
1½ C. shredded Cheddar cheese
1 (12 oz.) can sliced mushrooms
1 (6 oz.) can sliced black olives
¾ C. chopped ham
Sliced jalapeno peppers (optional)
12 eggs
½ C. milk
½ tsp. salt
Pepper to taste

Directions

Preheat oven to 350°. Melt butter in a small skillet over medium heat. Sauté onion until translucent. In a greased 9 x 13″ baking dish, layer cheese, mushrooms, olives, ham and, if desired, jalapenos. In a large bowl, beat together eggs, milk, salt and pepper. Pour egg mixture over ingredients in baking dish. Bake for 30 minutes or until center is set. Let stand for 10 minutes before serving.

Italian Brunch Bake

Ingredients

1 (8 oz.) pkg. sweet Italian sausage
1 C. sliced green onions
3 C. diced zucchini
1 tsp. salt
½ tsp. pepper
1 (7 oz.) jar roasted red bell peppers,
    drained and chopped
1 (1 lb.) Italian bread loaf, cut into 1″ cubes
2 C. shredded sharp Cheddar cheese
6 eggs
1½ C. milk

Directions

Preheat oven to 325°. Remove and discard casings from sausage. In a large skillet over medium-high heat, crumble and cook sausage until browned; drain grease. Stir in green onions, zucchini, salt and pepper. Sauté for approximately 5 minutes or until vegetables are tender. Stir in roasted bell peppers. Drain and cool mixture. In a greased 9 x 13″ baking dish, spread half of the bread cubes then layer with half of the sausage mixture and half of the cheese. Repeat layers. In a medium bowl, beat together eggs and milk. Pour egg mixture over ingredients in baking dish. Cover and refrigerate for 8 to 12 hours. Preheat oven to 325°. Bake for 1 hour. Let stand for 10 minutes before serving.

Creamy Ham & Hash Brown Casserole

Makes 12 servings

Ingredients
1 (32 oz.) pkg. frozen hash browns
1 C. diced ham
2 (10.75 oz.) cans cream of potato soup
1 (16 oz.) container sour cream
2 C. shredded sharp Cheddar cheese
1½ C. grated Parmesan cheese

Directions
Preheat oven to 375°. In a large bowl, combine hash browns, ham, potato soup, sour cream and Cheddar cheese. Spread mixture into a greased 9 x 13″ baking dish. Sprinkle with Parmesan cheese. Bake for 1 hour or until bubbly and light brown. Let stand for 10 minutes before serving.

Potluck Strata

Makes 12 servings

Ingredients

1 lb. sliced bacon, cut into ½" pieces
2 C. chopped ham
1 small onion, chopped
10 slices white bread, cubed
1 C. cubed cooked potatoes
3 C. shredded Cheddar cheese
8 eggs
3 C. milk
1 T. Worcestershire sauce
1 tsp. dry mustard
Salt and pepper to taste

Directions

In a large skillet over medium-high heat, cook bacon until crisp. Add ham and onion. Sauté until onion is translucent; drain grease. In a greased 9 x 13" baking dish, layer half of the bread cubes, half of the potatoes and half of the cheese. Top with all of the bacon mixture then repeat layers. In a medium bowl, beat together eggs, milk, Worcestershire sauce and dry mustard. Season with salt and pepper; pour over all. Cover and refrigerate for 8 to 12 hours. Remove from refrigerator and let stand for 30 minutes before baking. Preheat oven to 325°. Bake for 65 to 70 minutes or until center is set. Let stand for 10 minutes before serving.

Grits and Sausage Bake

Ingredients

1 lb. bulk pork sausage
3 C. water
¾ C. quick grits
2 C. (8 oz.) shredded sharp Cheddar cheese, divided
⅔ C. (5 oz. can) evaporated milk
¼ tsp. garlic powder
⅛ tsp. hot pepper sauce (optional)
2 large eggs, lightly beaten

Directions

Preheat oven to 350°. In a large skillet over medium-high heat, crumble and cook sausage until browned; set aside. In a medium saucepan, bring water to a boil then stir in grits. Cover and reduce heat to low. Cook, stirring occasionally, for 5 to 6 minutes. Add 1½ cups cheese, evaporated milk, garlic powder and hot pepper sauce. Stir until cheese is melted. Mix in sausage and eggs. Pour mixture into a greased 8″ square baking dish. Bake for 1 hour. Sprinkle with remaining ½ cup cheese. Bake for an additional 5 minutes or until cheese is melted. Let stand for 10 minutes before serving.

Potato Strata

Makes 8 servings

Ingredients

4 C. sliced potatoes
1 lb. bulk Italian sausage or bulk pork sausage
2 C. thinly sliced mushrooms
1 medium onion, chopped
2 cloves garlic, minced
1 T. all-purpose flour
½ tsp. salt
¼ tsp. white pepper
¼ tsp. ground nutmeg
1 C. milk
1 (15 oz.) carton ricotta cheese
1 (10 oz.) pkg. frozen chopped spinach,
    thawed and well-drained
½ C. grated Parmesan cheese
1 egg, slightly beaten
2 C. shredded mozzarella cheese, divided

Directions

Preheat oven to 350°. In a medium saucepan over medium-high heat, cook potatoes in a small amount of water for 5 minutes; set aside. In a large skillet over medium-high heat, crumble and cook sausage. Add mushrooms, onion and garlic. Sauté until sausage is browned. Drain grease then stir in flour, salt, pepper, nutmeg and milk. Cook and stir until thickened; set aside. In a medium bowl, combine ricotta, spinach, Parmesan and egg. In a greased 3-quart baking dish, layer half of the potatoes, half of the spinach mixture, half of the sausage mixture and 1 cup mozzarella cheese. Repeat layers except for the mozzarella. Bake, covered, for 25 minutes. Sprinkle with remaining 1 cup mozzarella. Bake for an additional 5 minutes.

Bayou Brunch

Makes 8 servings

Ingredients

4 oz. Italian sausage, casings removed
½ (1 lb.) loaf day-old French bread,
    broken into small chunks
3 T. butter or margarine, melted
1 lb. shredded Monterey Jack cheese
10 eggs
1½ C. whole milk
⅓ C. white wine
3 green onions, chopped
2 tsp. Dijon mustard
¼ tsp. pepper
¼ tsp. red pepper flakes
1 C. sour cream
½ C. grated Parmesan cheese

Directions

In a large skillet over medium-high heat, crumble and cook sausage until browned. Drain grease and set aside. Spread bread in a greased 9 x 13″ baking dish. Toss cubes with melted butter then layer sausage and Monterey Jack cheese over top. In a large bowl, beat together eggs, milk, wine, onions, mustard, pepper and red pepper flakes; pour over cheese. Cover dish and refrigerate for 8 to 12 hours. Remove from refrigerator and let stand for 30 minutes before baking. Preheat oven to 325°. Bake, covered, for 30 minutes. Uncover and bake for an additional 30 minutes. Remove from oven and spread sour cream and Parmesan over top. Bake for 10 minutes. Let stand for 10 minutes before serving.

Speedy Egg & Cheese Strata

Ingredients
6 eggs, beaten
6 (8 to 10″) flour tortillas, divided
1 C. shredded Mexican-style cheese
2 tomatoes, thinly sliced
Fresh cilantro
Chunky salsa (optional)

Directions
Preheat oven to 375°. In a medium greased skillet over medium heat, cook eggs, stirring often to scramble, for 5 minutes or until eggs are almost set. In a 9″ pie plate, overlap 2 tortillas. Top with a third of the eggs, a fourth of the cheese and a third of the tomato slices. Repeat layers two more times then top with remaining cheese and tomato slices; sprinkle with cilantro. Bake for 10 minutes. Let stand for 10 minutes before serving. If desired, serve with chunky salsa.

Tater Tot Breakfast Casserole

Makes 12 servings

Ingredients
1 lb. bulk pork sausage
12 eggs
1 (10.75 oz.) can cream of mushroom soup
1 (10.75 oz.) can milk
1 (4.5 oz.) can sliced mushrooms
1 (32 oz.) pkg. frozen tater tots
½ C. shredded Cheddar cheese

Directions
Preheat oven to 350°. In a large skillet over medium-high heat, crumble and cook sausage until browned. Drain grease and set aside. In a large bowl, beat together eggs, cream of mushroom soup and milk. Stir in sausage and mushrooms. Pour mixture into a greased 9 x 13″ baking dish. Mix in tater tots. Bake for 45 to 50 minutes. Sprinkle with cheese and bake for an additional 10 minutes or until cheese is melted. Let stand 10 minutes before serving.

Bacon, Broccoli & Egg Bake

Makes 12 servings

Ingredients

1 lb. sliced bacon
8 slices bread
2 T. butter or margarine, softened
2 C. shredded Cheddar cheese
1 (12 oz.) pkg. frozen broccoli florets
12 eggs
2 C. milk
½ tsp. dry mustard
⅛ tsp. garlic powder
½ tsp. onion powder
Salt and pepper to taste

Directions

Preheat oven to 325°. In a large skillet over medium-high heat, cook bacon until crisp; drain, crumble and set aside. Spread butter over bread slices. In a greased 9 x 13″ baking dish, layer bread slices, butter side up, cheese, bacon and broccoli. In a large bowl, beat together eggs, milk, dry mustard, garlic powder and onion powder. Season with salt and pepper. Pour egg mixture over broccoli. Bake for 60 minutes or until center is set. Let stand for 10 minutes before serving.

Quick-Fix Egg Puff

Makes 12 servings

Ingredients
¼ C. butter or margarine
12 eggs
½ C. all-purpose flour
1 tsp. baking powder
2 C. cottage cheese
4 C. shredded Monterey Jack cheese

Directions
Preheat oven to 350°. Place butter in a 9 x 13″ baking dish. Set dish in oven to preheat. Place eggs, flour and baking powder in a blender or food processor; blend for 1 minute or until smooth. Transfer mixture to a large bowl and fold in cottage cheese and Monterey Jack cheese. Remove dish from oven and pour egg mixture over melted butter. Bake for 30 minutes or until center is set. Let stand for 10 minutes before serving.

Roasted Veggie Hash & Eggs

Ingredients

4 medium potatoes, peeled and cut into ½" cubes
1 small red bell pepper, cut into ½" pieces
2 medium zucchini, cut into ¼" half circle pieces
1 medium yellow onion, cut into ½" pieces
3 T. olive oil
Salt and pepper to taste
1 lb. Roma or plum tomatoes, seeded and chopped
2 garlic cloves, minced
2 tsp. chopped fresh thyme
6 eggs
¼ C. grated Parmesan cheese

Directions

Preheat oven to 400°. On a lightly greased baking sheet, toss potato cubes, bell pepper, zucchini, onion and olive oil. Season with salt and pepper. Bake, stirring occasionally, for 40 minutes or until potatoes are almost tender. Stir in tomatoes, garlic and thyme. Bake for an additional 20 minutes. Transfer vegetables to a greased 2-quart baking dish. Break eggs evenly apart over vegetables; do not stir. Bake for an additional 10 minutes or until eggs are set. Sprinkle with cheese before serving.

Bed & Breakfast Casserole

Makes 8 servings

Ingredients
1 lb. bulk pork sausage
1 green onion, chopped
2 C. shredded Cheddar cheese
6 eggs, lightly beaten
1 C. water
½ C. milk
1 (2.64 oz.) pkg. country gravy mix
6 slices bread, cut into 1″ cubes
2 T. butter or margarine, melted
Paprika to taste (optional)

Directions
Preheat oven to 325°. In a large skillet over medium-high heat, crumble and cook sausage until browned; drain grease and set aside. In a greased 7 x 11″ baking dish, combine sausage and onion then top with cheese. In a medium bowl, beat together eggs, water, milk and gravy mix. Stir mixture into sausage mixture. Arrange bread cubes evenly over all. Drizzle melted butter over bread cubes. If desired, sprinkle with paprika. Bake for 40 minutes. Let stand for 10 minutes before serving.

Cornbread Casserole

Makes 8 servings

Ingredients

1 lb. bulk pork sausage
1 (16 oz.) pkg. dry cornbread mix
1 (15 oz.) can cream-style corn
½ C. plus 2 T. water
1 medium onion, diced
4 fresh jalapeno peppers, diced
2 C. shredded Cheddar-Monterey Jack cheese blend

Directions

Preheat oven to 350°. In a large skillet over medium-high heat, crumble and cook sausage until browned; drain grease and set aside. In a medium bowl, combine cornbread mix, corn and water. Cover the bottom of a greased 7 x 11" baking dish with ½" of the cornbread later. Layer sausage, onion, jalapeno and cheese over cornbread layer. Top with remaining cornbread mixture. Bake for 35 minutes. Let stand for 10 minutes before serving.

Make-Ahead Sourdough Strata

Makes 6 servings

Ingredients

1 tsp. butter or margarine
1½ C. vertically sliced onions
1⅓ C. finely chopped red bell pepper
¾ C. chopped Canadian bacon
6 C. (1″) cubed sourdough bread (about 12 oz.)
2 C. milk
1½ T. spicy brown mustard
¼ tsp. salt
¼ tsp. pepper
4 egg whites
2 eggs
1 C. shredded Swiss cheese

Directions

Melt butter in a large skillet over medium-high heat.
Sauté onions for 4 minutes, reduce heat and cook, stirring
occasionally, for an additional 10 minutes to caramelize
onions. Add bell pepper and cook for 1 minute. Stir in
Canadian bacon and remove from heat. In a greased
7 x 11″ baking dish, spread half of bread cubes and half
of onion mixture. Repeat layers. In a medium bowl, beat
milk, mustard, salt, pepper, egg whites and eggs. Pour
egg mixture into dish then top with cheese. Cover and
refrigerate for 8 to 12 hours. Remove dish and let stand for
30 minutes. Preheat oven to 375°. Bake, uncovered,
for 40 minutes. Let stand for 10 minutes before serving.

Amish Egg Bake

Makes 12 servings

Ingredients

1 lb. sliced bacon, cut to ½″ pieces
1 medium sweet onion, chopped
6 eggs
4 C. frozen shredded hash browns, thawed
2 C. shredded Cheddar cheese
1½ C. small curd cottage cheese
1¼ C. shredded Swiss cheese

Directions

Preheat oven to 350°. In a large skillet over medium-high heat, cook bacon and onion until bacon is crisp; drain grease. In a medium bowl, combine eggs, hash browns, Cheddar cheese, cottage cheese, Swiss cheese and bacon mixture. Pour into a greased 9 x 13″ baking dish. Bake, uncovered, for 35 to 40 minutes or until center is set. Let stand for 10 minutes before serving.

Cheesy Ham 'n' Potato Bake

Makes 10 servings

Ingredients

1 (24 oz.) pkg. frozen hash browns
2 C. cubed ham
¾ C. shredded Cheddar cheese, divided
1 small onion, chopped
2 C. sour cream
1 (10.75 oz.) can Cheddar cheese soup
1 (10.75 oz.) can cream of potato soup
¼ tsp. pepper

Directions

Preheat oven to 350°. In a large bowl, combine hash browns, ham, ½ cup cheese and onion. In a medium bowl, combine sour cream, Cheddar cheese soup, cream of potato soup and pepper. Add soup mixture to ham mixture then transfer to a greased 3-quart baking dish. Sprinkle with remaining ¼ cup cheese. Bake for 60 to 65 minutes. Let stand for 10 minutes before serving.

Southern Grits Casserole

Makes 16 servings

Ingredients

6 C. water
2 C. uncooked grits
½ C. butter or margarine, divided
3 C. shredded Cheddar cheese, divided
1 lb. bulk pork sausage
12 eggs
½ C. milk
Salt and pepper to taste

Directions

Preheat oven to 350°. In a large saucepan, bring water to a boil then stir in grits. Reduce heat, cover and simmer for 5 minutes. Stir in ¼ cup butter and 2 cups cheese until melted. In a large skillet over medium-high heat, crumble and cook sausage until browned. Drain grease and stir sausage into grits. In a large bowl, beat together eggs and milk. Season with salt and pepper. Add egg mixture to skillet and cook over medium heat, stirring often to scramble, until eggs are almost set. Stir eggs into grits mixture. Transfer to a greased 3-quart baking dish. Dot with remaining ¼ cup butter and 1 cup cheese. Bake for 30 minutes. Let stand for 10 minutes before serving.

Spinach Cheese Strata

Makes 6 servings

Ingredients

2 T. butter or margarine
½ C. chopped onion
¼ C. chopped sweet red bell pepper
¼ C. chopped green bell pepper
1 (10 oz.) pkg. frozen chopped spinach,
    thawed and well-drained
2 C. Wheat Chex cereal
½ C. shredded Cheddar cheese
½ C. shredded Swiss cheese
6 eggs
2 C. milk
⅓ C. crumbled cooked bacon
1 tsp. Dijon mustard
1 tsp. salt
¼ tsp. white pepper

Directions

Preheat oven to 325°. Melt butter in a large skillet over medium-high heat. Sauté onion and bell peppers until tender but crisp. Remove from heat and stir in spinach and cereal. Add mixture to a greased 7 x 11″ baking dish. Sprinkle both cheeses over mixture. In a medium bowl, beat together eggs, milk, bacon, mustard, salt and pepper. Pour over cheeses. Bake for 45 to 50 minutes or until center is set. Let stand for 10 minutes before serving.

This & That

Baked Bacon

Makes 6 servings

Ingredients

1 lb. thick-sliced bacon

Directions

Preheat oven to 375°. Arrange bacon in a single layer on a lightly greased foil-lined 10 x 15″ baking sheet. Bake for 10 minutes then flip bacon slices over and bake for an additional 7 to 15 minutes or until bacon is crisp. Transfer slices to paper towels to soak up grease before serving.

Brown Sugar Bacon

Makes 6 servings

Ingredients

1 lb. sliced hickory-smoked bacon
1 C. brown sugar
1 T. pepper

Directions

Preheat oven to 425°. Cut bacon slices in half. Combine brown sugar and pepper in a shallow bowl. Dredge bacon in mixture, shaking off excess. Arrange bacon in a single layer on a lightly greased foil-lined 10 x 15″ baking sheet. Bake for 10 minutes then flip bacon over and bake for an additional 7 to 15 minutes or until bacon is crisp.

Sweet Potato Hash

Makes 6 servings

Ingredients
4 C. diced peeled sweet potato
2 C. diced red potato
2 T. oil
1 C. diced Canadian bacon
1 C. chopped green bell pepper
⅔ C. chopped green onions
¾ tsp. salt
½ tsp. celery seed
½ tsp. pepper
⅛ tsp. ground nutmeg
¼ C. chicken broth
1 T. cider vinegar

Directions
In a large saucepan over medium-high heat, place sweet and red potatoes; cover with water. Bring water to a boil then reduce heat and simmer for 5 minutes. Drain saucepan and set aside. Heat oil in a large skillet over medium heat. Cook Canadian bacon, stirring often, for 4 minutes. Add bell pepper and green onions; continue cooking, stirring often, for 2 minutes. Add potatoes, salt, celery seed, pepper and nutmeg; continue cooking, stirring occasionally, for 4 minutes. Stir in broth and vinegar until well combined.

Cherry & Pecan Oatmeal

Makes 6 servings

Ingredients
3 C. water
3 C. milk
2 C. whole oats (instant will not work)
½ C. dried cherries, coarsely chopped
½ tsp. salt
¼ C. brown sugar
1 T. butter or margarine
¼ tsp. cinnamon
¼ tsp. vanilla
2 T. chopped pecans, toasted*

Directions
In a large saucepan over medium-high heat, combine water, milk, whole oats, cherries and salt. Bring mixture to a boil then reduce heat and simmer, stirring occasionally, for 20 minutes or until it reaches desired consistency. Stir in brown sugar, butter, cinnamon and vanilla. Sprinkle each serving with pecans.

To toast pecans, evenly coat nuts with melted butter. Spread pecans in an even layer on a baking sheet. Bake at 350° for 10 to 15 minutes, tossing once or twice while baking to ensure pecans are evenly toasted. Watch carefully to be sure pecans don't burn!

Breakfast Patties

Makes 6 servings

Ingredients
2 tsp. dried sage
2 tsp. salt
1 tsp. pepper
¼ tsp. dried marjoram
1 T. brown sugar
⅛ tsp. red pepper flakes
1 pinch ground cloves
2 lbs. ground pork

Directions
In a small bowl, mix sage, salt, pepper, marjoram, brown sugar, red pepper flakes and cloves. In a large bowl, add the ground pork then mix in spice mixture. Use your hands to thoroughly combine spices and meat then form mixture into patties. In a large skillet over medium-high heat, fry patties for 5 minutes then flip and continue cooking for an additional 5 minutes.

Biscuits & Sausage Gravy

Ingredients
1 (12 oz.) pkg. maple-flavored sausage
3 T. butter or margarine
¼ C. all-purpose flour
3 C. whole milk
Salt and pepper to taste
Prepared biscuits, your choice

Directions
In a large skillet over medium-high heat, crumble and cook sausage until browned. Remove sausage from pan, reserving drippings, and set aside. Add the butter and stir until melted. Stir in flour until smooth. Reduce heat to medium and continue to cook until mixture is a light brown color. Slowly add milk, whisking as you pour. Continue cooking until thickened. Season with salt and pepper. Stir in cooked sausage. Reduce heat and simmer for 12 to 15 minutes. Serve over biscuits of your choice.

Tex-Mex Eggs Benedict

Makes 4 servings

Ingredients
4 slices Canadian bacon
1½ C. picante sauce
½ tsp. ground cumin
4 eggs
2 (3 oz.) pkgs. cream cheese, cubed
2 English muffins, split and toasted
1 T. chopped fresh cilantro

Directions
In a small skillet, cook Canadian bacon on both sides until hot and lightly browned; set aside. In a medium skillet over low heat, combine picante sauce and cumin. Add eggs, one at a time, and fry on both sides until cooked to desired doneness. Remove eggs from skillet, cover with foil and set aside. Add cream cheese to skillet and stir until mixture is melted and well combined. To serve, top each muffin half with 1 slice Canadian bacon, 1 fried egg and some of the sauce. Sprinkle with fresh cilantro.

Hearty Breakfast Hash

Ingredients
2 lbs. potatoes, cubed
½ lb. sliced bacon
1 green bell pepper, seeded and julienne-cut
1 red bell pepper, seeded and julienne-cut
1 onion, sliced
2 C. sliced mushrooms
Salt and pepper to taste
3 C. shredded American cheese
8 eggs

Directions
In a large saucepan over high heat, place potatoes and cover with water. Bring water to a boil then reduce heat and simmer until potatoes are tender but firm. Drain water and set aside. In a large skillet over medium-high heat, cook bacon until crisp. Remove bacon, reserving drippings. Cool and crumble bacon; set aside. Add potato cubes to skillet and sauté, stirring occasionally, until browned. Add bell peppers, onion and mushrooms. Cook, stirring occasionally, until vegetables are tender but firm. Stir in bacon. Season with salt and pepper. Reduce heat to low and sprinkle with cheese, stirring to melt. In a large skillet, add eggs one at a time, frying on both sides to desired doneness. To serve, divide hash onto 4 plates then top each serving with 2 eggs.

South-of-the-Border Bacon & Eggs Pizza

Makes 6 servings

Ingredients
12 slices bacon
6 eggs
¼ C. milk
¼ C. sliced green onions
1 (11") Italian pizza crust
½ C. chunky mild salsa
1 C. shredded Mexican-style cheese, divided

Directions
Preheat oven to 400°. In a large skillet over medium-high heat, cook bacon until crisp; drain grease and set aside. In a medium bowl, beat eggs, milk and green onions. In a medium greased skillet over medium heat, cook eggs, stirring occasionally to scramble. Place pizza crust on a baking sheet. Spread salsa evenly over crust. Layer ½ cup cheese, ⅔ crumbled bacon and egg mixture over salsa. Sprinkle with remaining cheese and crumbled bacon. Bake for 10 minutes or until cheese is melted.

Cheesy Baked Grits

Makes 6 to 8 servings

Ingredients
5 C. chicken broth
1¼ C. uncooked quick-cooking grits
1 C. shredded extra-sharp Cheddar cheese
1 C. shredded Monterey Jack cheese
¼ C. whipping cream
1 tsp. hot sauce
¼ tsp. pepper
⅛ to ¼ tsp. ground red pepper
1 tsp. Worcestershire sauce
3 eggs, lightly beaten

Directions
Preheat oven to 350°. In a medium saucepan over medium-high heat, bring broth to a boil. Slowly add grits, whisking until well combined. Return mixture to a boil then reduce heat to medium-low and simmer, stirring occasionally, for 10 minutes or until thickened. Stir in cheese, cream, hot sauce, pepper, red pepper and Worcestershire sauce. Continue cooking and stirring until cheese melts. Remove mixture from heat and stir in eggs. Pour grits in a lightly greased 2-quart baking dish. Bake for 40 to 45 minutes or until center is set and golden.

Coconut Oatmeal

Makes 6 servings

Ingredients

3½ C. milk
¼ tsp. salt
2 C. old-fashioned oats
¼ C. maple syrup
⅓ C. raisins
⅓ C. dried cranberries
⅓ C. sweetened flaked coconut
⅓ C. chopped walnuts
1 (8 oz.) container plain yogurt (optional)
3 T. honey (optional)

Directions

In a medium saucepan over medium heat, combine milk and salt. Bring mixture to a boil, stirring often, then add oats, syrup, raisins and cranberries. Once mixture begins to boil again, reduce heat to medium and continue cooking for 5 minutes. Stir in coconut and walnuts. Remove from heat and let oatmeal stand until it reaches desired consistency. If desired, serve with a topping of yogurt and honey.

Baked Apple-Nut Oatmeal

Ingredients
4 C. milk
½ C. brown sugar
2 tsp. butter or margarine
½ tsp. salt
½ tsp. cinnamon
2 C. old-fashioned oats
2 C. chopped, peeled apples
1 C. chopped walnuts
1 C. raisins
1 C. wheat germ

Directions
Preheat oven to 350°. In a medium saucepan over medium heat, combine milk, brown sugar, butter, salt and cinnamon. Add oats, apples, walnuts, raisins and wheat germ; mix until combined. Pour mixture into a greased 2-quart baking dish. Cover and bake for 45 minutes.

Homestyle Fried Potatoes

Makes 4 servings

Ingredients
4 red potatoes
3 T. olive oil, divided
1 onion, chopped
1 green bell pepper, seeded and diced
1 tsp. salt
¾ tsp. paprika
¼ tsp. pepper
¼ C. chopped fresh parsley

Directions
Place potatoes in a large saucepan over medium-high heat; add enough water to cover potatoes. Bring water to a boil and cook until potatoes are tender but firm. Drain saucepan. Cool potatoes and cut into cubes; set aside. Heat 1 tablespoon olive oil in a large skillet over medium-high heat. Sauté onion and bell pepper, stirring often, for 5 minutes. Transfer to a plate and set aside. Heat remaining 2 tablespoons olive oil in skillet over medium-high heat. Add potato cubes, salt, paprika and pepper. Cook, stirring occasionally, for 10 minutes or until potatoes are golden brown. Stir in sautéed vegetables and parsley; continue to cook for another minute or until warmed through.

Index

Breakfast Anytime

Index

Breakfast Anytime

Index

Breakfast Anytime